Worth Thinking About?

Great thinkers through the ages have consists not simply of chasing happine are many times when we are not happy status or condition. Instead, these thinkers have suggested that we should seek out meaning and purpose in life.

The questions in this book are about the big issues of our existence – those issues which are often raised when considering that meaning for our lives which is offered by religious faith.

For each section there are questions which are designed to help you examine your own core beliefs and the underlying assumptions which you hold.

Dip into the questions in any order. All of them stand on their own, though some are interrelated.

Take your time – these questions go deep. Don't feel that you have to tackle them all at once – you are not in an exam! Maybe one question a day would be a good idea – perhaps with a cup of coffee.

In many cases you will be able to spot what aspect of the issue a question is addressing, but you can also check the text at the end of each section for further guidance. You will not find ready-made answers, but you will see some of the thinking behind the questions so that you can go further into the issues.

Finally, remember:

All doubts . . . are really a set of alternative beliefs.

So, if you say what you don't believe, you should be able to say what you do believe instead. And you should be able to support this with evidence, because:

An assertion is not an argument!

Reverend Peter Hopkins
Great Gonerby Rectory

GOD 60 Hard Questions for Sceptics

Contents

Methods & Assumptions
1 Truth and Proof 5

Scientific Questions
2 Existence of God 9
3 Science 13
4 Psychology 17

Lifestyle Questions
5 Freedom 21
6 Tolerance 25

Ethical Questions
7 Morality 27
8 Religious Violence 31
9 Christian Behaviour 33
10 Suffering 35

Questions about Christianity
11 Exclusive Claims 37
12 Biblical Reliability 39
13 Jesus Christ 43

One Final Question 45

GOD

60 Hard Questions for Sceptics

Reverend Peter Hopkins

First published in 2019
by Autumn House Publications (Europe) Ltd.

All rights reserved.
No part of this publication may be reproduced
in any form without prior permission from the publisher.

British Library Cataloguing in Publication Data.
A catalogue record for this book
is available from the British Library.

ISBN: 978-1-78665-947-7

Designed by Abigail Murphy.

Printed in Serbia.

Truth & Proof

Methods & Assumptions

> We all hold a worldview – a set of basic beliefs and principles which determine how we choose to live. Our worldview may be traditionally religious or nonreligious. It may be a mix of ideas and influences drawn from different sources. How do we test our worldview against the alternatives available?
>
> It's necessary that we get our thinking straight on this topic before we tackle the issues in the rest of the book.

5 Questions

1. How do we decide what is true?

2. Can we each agree to have our own truths, or is there such a thing as absolute truth?

3. Is our view of what is true determined by our upbringing and culture?

4. Is there anyone, religious or non-religious, who is completely neutral, unbiased, and objective in their thinking?

GOD 60 Hard Questions for Sceptics

5 Whatever views you have about life, God, and the universe, do you hold these beliefs because you feel you have:
a) 100% proof;
b) Reasonable evidence;
c) Common-sense intuition?

1 Truth & Proof

1 We assess truth by how well we think it fits the evidence or data which we have available. For example, when scientists agree that a theory makes sense of all the data they have collected on a topic it is deemed to be true (at least until a better-fitting theory comes along!).

This method is not limited to science. We use it in everyday life. We ask ourselves, 'What are the facts?' and, 'Does what I have heard (or read, or watched) fit the facts as I understand them?'

Discerning the truth will mean considering and rejecting opposing alternative theories as we look for the one that fits best.

2 Relative truth is a popular idea nowadays. It suggests that a person subscribing to the idea is benevolent and broad-minded. But when one truth contradicts another, then only one of them can be correct. If we pretend that both can be correct it is not really helpful, and deep down we probably don't believe it ourselves.

Whether we realise it or not, we live with absolute truth almost all the time.

Yet we tend to be suspicious of absolute truth claims perhaps because they make us feel controlled. We want to be free, to be critical thinkers with open minds.

Truth & Proof

Methods & Assumptions

3 Our beliefs will differ depending on our backgrounds, but that doesn't mean that the truth changes. Someone born in North Korea would probably hold atheistic beliefs – but that doesn't make atheism true. In seeking what is true we may need to be countercultural.

4 Non-religious thinkers often assume that they occupy a neutral space of freethinking: but there is no such neutral space. Non-religious thinkers have got their own presuppositions just as much as people of religious faith. If you wish to compare and criticise other worldviews, you need to be aware of the unproven assumptions in your own position.

Common assumptions would include, for example, the propositions that there is nothing which cannot be explained in terms of the physical/material world and that miracles do not happen.

(Because this question underpins all our thinking it is an important key in opening up the questions in this book.)

5 There is an idea held by some modern atheists (including Richard Dawkins) that we cannot believe anything which cannot be proved 100%. This 'strong rationalism', as it is called, is one reason that Dawkins' books are criticised – even by fellow atheists. 'Strong rationalism' is impossible to uphold. We all come to our decisions with all sorts of experiences and background beliefs that strongly influence how we think and how we reason. *'Even Dawkins lives more by faith than by reason. We hold many beliefs that have no unimpeachable rational justification, but are nonetheless reasonable to entertain.'* Terry Eagleton – Marxist scholar.[1]

Outside of pure mathematics, we don't talk about

GOD 60 Hard Questions for Sceptics

'proof' in this strict sense. Even in a court of law, jury members are asked to make their decisions not on 100% proof of guilt and innocence, but on proof 'beyond reasonable doubt'.

Most of our life decisions, big and small, are taken on balance of probabilities, yet when discussing the existence of God people often demand that it be proven 100%. Isn't this unreasonable? Shouldn't we be looking to accept cumulative reasonable evidence?

> *'If someone tells you there is no such thing as (absolute) truth they are asking you not to believe them – so don't.'* Roger Scruton, philosopher

Existence of God 2

Can a reasonably intelligent person believe in a supreme being? What, if any, evidence is there to convince us of the existence of such a being?

Many people, particularly in Western societies, find it difficult to accept the existence of a supreme being. They maintain that evidence is severely lacking.

6 Questions

1. If you think there is not enough evidence to prove the existence of God, what more evidence might you need?

2. In what ways might it be unfair, or harmful for us, if God were to 'force' us to believe in Him by openly showing Himself to us?

3. If God exists, what might be the risks associated with ignoring His existence?

4. There are many things that stop people believing in God which are not concerned with logic and evidence. Maybe they've had a bad experience in the past.

GOD 60 Hard Questions for Sceptics

Is it your reason, or is it something else which is your stumbling block to faith?

5 Would you like God to exist . . . or not?

6 Do you think there may be clues which, though falling short of absolute proof, may nevertheless support belief in the existence of God?

2 Existence of God

2 The seventeenth-century philosopher and mathematician Blaise Pascal developed the 'just enough light' principle: that is, if God gave less light, true seekers would not find Him; if God gave more light even the indifferent would find Him, against their will. This would amount to coercion – forcing people to believe. But God respects the will and freedom of all. So God offers us just enough evidence to make an informed decision.

3 If we take the approach that we feel no need for God and are not interested in thinking about the subject, we are betting our life on the hope that no God exists who would hold us accountable for our beliefs and our behaviour. Isn't this quite a risky leap of faith?

4, 5 Pascal also thought that, although we like to think that we make our life decisions on pure reason, in fact, most of the time, emotion and imagination heavily influence our decisions. (This is not a problem as long as we recognise this – after all, we don't want to be like Mr Spock in *Star Trek*.) Pascal used his 'plank' example to

Existence of God

Scientific Questions

illustrate this. Put a plank down on the ground and ask someone to walk across it – no problem. Now put the same plank across a 100m-deep chasm. Our reason would say it is still easy to walk across. Our emotions and imagination might say something else!

6 Question 6 is based on the idea that although we cannot absolutely prove God (but review section 1.1 – *Truth and Proof*), nevertheless there are many strong clues which, taken together, may make a good case for God's existence.

Accepting the existence of God may fit what we are discovering about the universe better than any other worldview.

For example, almost all scientists now accept that the universe, and time itself, has not been going forever (as was previously believed), but had a beginning in what is called 'The Big Bang'. Could God have been the cause, or is there some other explanation?

Similarly, scientists know that tiny changes to some physical constants in the universe (for example, the force of gravity and the speed of light, among many others) would have 'aborted' the creation of the universe and made life on Earth impossible. How would you explain this precision?

'A common-sense interpretation of the facts suggests that some super intellect has monkeyed with physics, and that there are no blind forces worth speaking about in nature.' Sir Fred Hoyle, scientist

GOD 60 Hard Questions for Sceptics

Science

Scientific Questions

Nowadays, technology plays a big part in our everyday lives. Because science is continually making new discoveries about our physical world, it is viewed as the only way to understand our existence. Belief in God is often seen as opposed to an acceptance of science.

4 Questions

1. Do science and religious faith have to be opposed to each other?

2. Some people think that religious faith is based on empty assertions and, by contrast, non-religious thinking is based on proven facts. Do you agree?

3. Is science the only valid form of knowledge?

4. If science has disproved God, then why do more scientists have a religious faith than people in many other professions – for example, journalists or entertainers?

GOD 60 Hard Questions for Sceptics

> 'The odds against a universe like ours emerging out of something like the Big Bang are enormous. I think there are clearly religious implications.'
> 'It would be very difficult to explain why the universe would have begun in just this way except as the act of a God who intended to create beings like us.' Stephen Hawking, scientist[2]

The problem comes when people decide that science can also do philosophy!

3 Science

1 The percentage of trained scientists who believe in God is about the same as for the population as a whole. They do not, in general, see a problem between their science and their religion. Science is not the enemy of Christianity, but sometimes people refuse to accept that the physical sciences might not have all the answers. Christians don't use God as an explanation for what they don't currently understand, but rather as the best explanation of what they do understand.

2, 3 Even if you try to explain all of life in terms of science, you will find that you will still have to make some assumptions that are just not provable by science. This is because, while science can help us to explain much about how the world works, there are many questions that science is not equipped to answer: for example, questions about human character and emotions, morality, and God. In these cases we have to look to

Science

other forms of knowledge – such as philosophy and human experience.

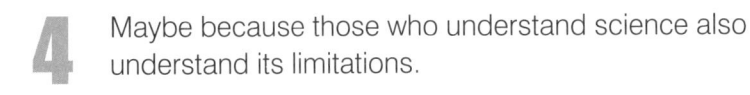

4 Maybe because those who understand science also understand its limitations.

> *'Religion without science is lame; science without religion is blind.'* Albert Einstein

GOD 60 Hard Questions for Sceptics

Psychology

Psychology 4

Scientific Questions

Is religious faith merely a sort of comfort blanket that provides support through life's difficulties?
Is it 'all in the head'?

6 Questions

1 Should children be taught about faith?

2 Is all religion brainwashing?

3 Do you think all people's experiences of God are delusional?

4 Is God a crutch for those who need comfort and support?

5 Is it always a sign of weakness if we accept the help of others?

6 Many people make use of things that enable them to live or perform better. Is this wrong?

GOD 60 Hard Questions for Sceptics

Psychology

1 Non-religious people sometimes object to religious people passing on their beliefs to children. However, atheism is also a belief which many pass on to their children.

Each person must make their own free choice – and choice implies that both sides of the argument are presented and considered.

2 Powerful leaders can and have used religion to control or manipulate people – but that does not imply that all religion is brainwashing. Non-religious worldviews have been manipulated to the same end.

3 Some people's experience may be delusional. It is a matter of weighing all the available evidence.

4 *'If believing in God makes you happy – that's fine!'*
The idea that God is a psychological projection invented to fill a gap in the lives of weaker individuals can be argued the other way. You could say that atheists may have psychological baggage which makes them wary of trusting anyone else for support – even when it helps.

5, 6 It is false to assume that those who find their relationship with God practical, meaningful and effective must be weak and inferior individuals just because they rely on something outside of themselves.

Psychology

> 'If belief in God makes sense of the world and provides a positive moral framework that helps people to live constructively, that is not a reason to disbelieve in Him. Similarly, if a relationship with God enables the believer to find healing, wholeness and comfort in the midst of human suffering, we should not be surprised. After all, if God is real, His existence will have a massive impact on life and on the experience of life.'[3]

GOD 60 Hard Questions for Sceptics

Freedom

Freedom 5

All religions have their rules and conventions. Do these prevent a person from living a truly free life?

3 Questions

1 'True freedom is freedom to create your own meaning and purpose.' Do you agree with this statement?

2 Is freedom simply the rejection of constraints?

3 Many people would say they are 'spiritual' but do not want to take on the beliefs and practice of a religion. Why do you think this is?

5 Freedom

1, 2 When a couple love each other, they each agree to give up part of their freedom and their independence for the sake of their relationship. Freedom is not so much the absence of restrictions as finding the right restrictions – those which liberate.

GOD 60 Hard Questions for Sceptics

Freedom

When we join a club or society we choose to restrict our freedom in order to gain the enjoyment of whatever that society offers. This is also true of faith – we agree to restrict our freedom because of the ultimate greater gain.

3 Nowadays there is a growing distrust in large and powerful organisations, whether these be governments, political bodies or business corporations. There is a feeling that these are working against, rather than for, the 'ordinary person', and these feelings are supported by media reports of various scandals and self-seeking behaviour. This distrust is also carried over to the large religious organisations, and so people have opted for forms of do-it-yourself spirituality and self-improvement which they hope will meet their spiritual needs without carrying the stigma of 'organised religion'.

C. S. Lewis was once approached by a retired military officer who told him that, while he had no use for all the stuff of organised religion, he was a religious person who knew there was a God. He had felt Him when out alone in the desert at night: a tremendous mystery.

Lewis explains that, while the man probably did have a real and exciting experience of God, such isolated experiences are of limited value – they lead nowhere.

Religious doctrine is like a map made up of the individual spiritual experiences of millions of people. Just as a map is only a piece of coloured paper and cannot compare to being out in the countryside, or climbing a mountain, so the doctrine may seem restrictive and dull. Yet, just as the map is the key to great country walks, so organised religion and teaching is the key to a progressively greater life experience of God and all the spiritual experiences which will flow from knowing Him.

Freedom

Lifestyle Questions

> *'I have no need of friendship;*
> *Friendship causes pain;*
> *Its laughter and its loving I disdain;*
> *I am a rock; I am an island.'*
> Paul Simon

> *'You will know the truth,*
> *and the truth will set you free.'*
> Jesus

GOD 60 Hard Questions for Sceptics

Tolerance

Tolerance is held up as one of the key virtues of our Western society.
Isn't there a danger that holding to a religious faith teaches a person to be intolerant of others?

4 Questions

1. What does tolerance mean to you?

2. 'In order to exercise tolerance, we first need to find someone with whom we strongly disagree.' Is this true?

3. Does tolerance mean accepting that all religions or worldviews are equally true or untrue?

4. Is it wrong to say to people that their ideas are wrong?

6 Tolerance

1-3 Many people misunderstand the virtue of tolerance to mean that we mustn't disagree with other people: but we can only practise tolerance when we have found people with whom we do disagree. If two people agree that one person's path leads to God as much as the other's, they don't need to be tolerant because they both agree. It is only if they disagree that they need to be tolerant towards each other.

Rather than practising this 'true tolerance', people instead seek to avoid conflict by agreeing to accept mutually incompatible ideas. They agree that 'I have my truth and you can have your truth – and that's okay'.

In some cases this may be acceptable, but if the ideas patently contradict each other, as they so often do when belief systems are compared, then this is not a sensible option.

4 This is a trick question. A person answering 'yes' has fallen into the trap of telling other people that their ideas are wrong!

Morality

Ethical Questions — **7**

*In this section we look at our ideas of right and wrong.
Where do these ideas come from?
Are they God-given or the products of human thought?*

8 Questions

1 Should we keep our religion private, and not allow it to influence decisions in the public arena: for example, government and law-making?

2 Are there people in the world who are doing things that you consider to be wrong?

3 Is it right for you to impose your moral views on others?

4 How do you decide what is good and what is evil?

5 Most people still have strong ideas of what is right and wrong. Why? Is there some kind of universal moral standard?
   If so, where is this from?

GOD 60 Hard Questions for Sceptics

6 The natural world is ruled by violence. If this is natural, why is the use of violence by the strong against the weak considered wrong in humans?

7 Why should the majority in a society consider the needs of minorities? Isn't this always against their own interests?

8 Shouldn't your own life and happiness be the only criteria for your decisions and actions?

7 Morality

1 Everyone has a worldview. Even the non-believer makes decisions based upon their own worldview and assumptions. A religion is a set of beliefs that explain what life is all about, who we are, and the most important things that human beings should spend their time doing. Faith in some view of the world and human nature informs everyone's life, whether it is consciously thought about or not. For example, the belief that people are more valuable than machines is an article of faith that is based on a religious stance.

2-4 These address the question of whether moral ideas are relative to a particular culture – for example, Western morality, Islamic morality, Nazi morality – or whether there are universal moral laws that should apply to every society.

Morality

5 If the answer to this question is yes, then we must ask how we get this universal moral standard. Who has set the rules?

6 One possible answer is based on evolution and nature. Those groups who worked together unselfishly were able to survive better than other groups. We, the descendants of those successful survivors, now have embedded in our genes the notion that unselfish behaviour is 'right'.

However, for evolutionary purposes, the opposite behaviour – hostility to all people outside one's group – could be considered to work in the group's interest. Evolution cannot account for the origin of our moral feelings and obligations.

If we look at nature, violence seems natural, so we cannot get our ideas of morality from the natural world.

7 Some people consider that a universal morality may come about because communities realise that this is the best way for them to thrive. But there has never been total agreement in human societies. Yet there is a feeling among the majority that they should respect the human rights of the minorities, even if it does not produce the most efficient society. If morality doesn't come from a consensus of the majority, where does it come from?

8 The nineteenth-century atheist philosopher Nietzsche argued that if there were no God then there could be no universal standards of morality. Good is simply that which enables one to fulfil one's potential, and evil is whatever stands in the way of this. Our own life and happiness are the only considerations when deciding what to do and how to behave. There are no good reasons to be compassionate and peaceful.

Few of us consistently follow Nietzsche's principles. Even those who deny that there is a God still seem to want to live as if God exists.

Religious Violence

Religious Violence 8

It's a common idea that 'religion is the cause of all wars'.
Is this really the case, and, if so, why might this be?

3 Questions

1 Try to list ten wars that have been fought in the last 200 years that were not about religion.

2 Of the 'religious' wars, which ones do you think were really about religious issues as opposed to, for example, national land grabs or bids for personal power and wealth?

3 Is all religious fanaticism bad, even if it is non-violent? In what situations might it be justified?

8 Religious Violence

1 In the last hundred years the greatest oppression and loss of life has been caused by secular, atheistic governments.

GOD 60 Hard Questions for Sceptics

Religious Violence

It seems that non-religious societies (for example, Soviet Russia, Communist China, the Cambodian Khmer Rouge, Nazi Germany, North Korea) are just as oppressive as religious ones (or more so). Can war and violence be tied to any worldview, or is it a symptom of the human condition?

2 Though many that are labelled as such have much more complex causes, there have been some genuinely 'religious' wars. These shortcomings can be understood historically as failures by the church to properly practise Christian principles. Rather than being used as arguments against Christianity, they could be seen as arguments for more real Christianity. It isn't against the tenets of atheism to make war and practise violence – whereas these things do go against Christian ethics.

3 Doesn't it depend on the religion (or the non-religion)? What about being fanatical for peace, or for love? Fundamentalism is nowadays used as a term of abuse: yet fundamentalism – defined as the act of merely returning to the fundamental principles of a belief system – is, in and of itself, neutral. In a sense, most of the traditional believers of the world's religions can be labelled 'fundamentalist'.

However, if fundamentalism involves intolerance of others, Christians should reject it *(but see the section on the meaning of tolerance).*

Christian Behaviour

Christian Behaviour 9

Is it right to accuse Christians of thinking that they are better than other people?
Are they?

3 Questions

1 Isn't it better to set a high standard of behaviour and sometimes fail than have no standard at all?

2 Is it reasonable to expect all Christians to be better people than all non-Christians?

3 In the past some people would have attended church for social reasons – for example, the squire or the mill owner attended – and so some people either had to attend or felt it would be to their advantage to do so.
Do you think that is the case today?

9 Christian Behaviour

1-3 If they are true followers of Jesus, then knowing Jesus should transform people – but not everyone starts from the same moral baseline.

In the gospels, we read that many 'disreputable' people followed Jesus because they understood that at the centre of His teaching was the message of forgiveness and the offer of a new start in life. They knew that they needed these things, unlike many of the religious people who already felt they were good enough for God. A person may have 'improved' on the moral scale but their life may still not compare well against some non-religious people.

In his book, *Mere Christianity*, C. S. Lewis makes the point that, although 'goodness' and a well-balanced personality are commendable, they are not what God is principally looking for in a person. These things largely come from our genetics and our upbringing. Some people are born with a pleasing disposition, others less so! We cannot claim these gifts to be of our own making and efforts.

What God is looking for are people who, of their own free will, choose to turn to Him. These people may be from the 'nasty' ones – or the 'nice' ones. Wherever they are on the moral scale, once they have offered their lives to Him, then God can begin to help them become the people they (and those around them!) would truly like to be. For some, however, this may take a lifetime and beyond.

Suffering 10

The question of suffering is one of the biggest challenges made to people of faith.
If God is all-powerful and good, then surely He could stop suffering, and would wish to do so.

4 Questions

1 How much suffering is caused by humans and could be stopped if we worked together to help each other?

2 How do you explain all the suffering that you see in the world?

3 Could suffering ever serve a positive purpose?

4 How much reduction in world suffering would you require before you would believe in God?

GOD 60 Hard Questions for Sceptics

Suffering

1 From war to travelling in aeroplanes, a great deal of world suffering is human-caused. Even some of it which is not (for example, tsunamis) could have its effects alleviated if we devoted sufficient resources.

However, there is still the question of those events which are not caused by humans – for example, childhood diseases. Why does God allow these?

2 The question of suffering is a challenge for all worldviews. We need to ask, 'Which worldview best answers the question and has the resources to handle human suffering?'

Christianity is realistic about suffering. It diagnoses the problem of evil and speaks of a God who acts in the world and comes alongside us in our suffering. It teaches that, in Christ, God came to earth and deliberately exposed Himself to human suffering.

3 Looking back through their lives, people can sometimes see good reasons for some of their sufferings.

4 Sometimes people use the suffering question purely as a philosophical means of justifying their desire not to believe in God. This question challenges that approach. So, would the person consider believing in God if, say, there were no childhood diseases, or cancer, or dementia, or disability . . . or even death?

Exclusive Claims

Exclusive Claims 11

> Are Christians behaving arrogantly in the claims they make for the uniqueness of their faith?

4 Questions

1. Is it wrong to be exclusive – that is, to claim your way is the only right one?

2. Do all paths lead to God?

3. Why should Christians be considered arrogant and intolerant for claiming that Christianity is the only true belief?

4. Why is it okay to say, 'I've found the best ever washing powder', but not okay to say, 'I've found the best belief system'?

11 Exclusive Claims

1. Every community is exclusive to some extent. For example, the rules of a football club would exclude

GOD 60 Hard Questions for Sceptics

Exclusive Claims

someone from joining who would sometimes like to pick up the ball and run with it. Each community defines itself by its particular rules and practices. This in itself does not make a group exclusive. It depends upon the nature of the exclusion, which can be narrow and oppressive.

2 Many people believe that all the major religions are basically the same. Well, yes, they are mostly about God, so in that sense they have a passing similarity. However, as soon as you start to compare them in any degree of detail it becomes clear that they are fundamentally very different. For example, neither Buddhism, Hinduism nor Islam contains the idea of a close relationship with God. In Christianity, knowing God personally and regarding Him as 'Our Father' is at the heart of the faith.

The person who says that all paths lead to God is declaring that they have better spiritual vision than Jesus, Buddha, Mohammed and Moses combined. This is not very humble.

3 All worldviews exclude other worldviews. Isn't it unreasonable to single out Christianity for being arrogant? By definition, atheism assumes that all people in all religions are wrong and that only atheists have the truth.

4 It does seem that sharing spiritual matters is often frowned upon, whereas sharing anything else in life is okay.

'All religions are the same. . . . They all believe in love and goodness. They only differ on matters of creation, sin, heaven, hell, God and salvation.' Steve Turner, poet

Biblical Reliability

Biblical Reliability 12

The Bible is a very old book, and it contains many references to miracles and supernatural events. Can we take it seriously?

7 Questions

1. Do you have a problem with miracles? Why is this?

2. Do you think the gospel accounts of Jesus' life are made-up stories?

3. Do you have problems with the Bible/gospels because you think it is inaccurate history?

4. How many ancient documents recording the activities of: (a) Julius Caesar in Gaul; (b) Jesus Christ do you think we have from before AD 900? None, 10, 50, or 5,000?

5. How long after Jesus' life do you think the New Testament documents were first written: 20 years, 100 years, or 1,000 years?

Questions about Christianity

GOD 60 Hard Questions for Sceptics

6 In the New Testament, the leaders of the early Christian Church are portrayed as fearful, dim, argumentative and cowardly. If the New Testament were a propaganda document to promote the early church, what advantage would the writers have for doing this?

7 Jesus' resurrection from the grave is, perhaps, the key event of the New Testament and Christianity. Given that in those times the testimony of women to any event was not even admissible as evidence in court, why would the writers have used women as the initial witnesses of this event?

12 Biblical Reliability

1 If God exists, why should there be a problem with miracles?

2-4 The first stage in assessing the trustworthiness of the New Testament (or any other ancient document) is to ask: does the document we read today have the same content as the original document? Has it been altered over the hundreds or thousands of years? Compared to other documents from the classical era the New Testament has a vastly greater base of documentary evidence.

For example, there are no documents of Julius Caesar's *Gallic Wars* existing from before AD 900. (Caesar lived just before Jesus Christ.) By comparison there are around 5,000 pieces of the New Testament

Biblical Reliability

scriptures dating from the first 500 years after Jesus Christ, with the earliest going back to around AD 100.

A short gap between the original and the first surviving manuscript presents a very small historical window for any alterations to have been made. Also, having such a large number of manuscripts allows them to be compared. There is a 99.6% correlation in the 24,000+ manuscripts of the New Testament which we now hold. If there had been many changes, then, when the copies were compared there would have been significant differences.

'Indeed, many ancient historians will count themselves fortunate to have four such responsible accounts, written within a generation or two of the events, and preserved in such a wealth of early manuscript evidence as to be, from the point of view of textual criticism, virtually uncontested in all the detail.' R. T. France, Bible scholar[4]

5 The second stage in assessing the trustworthiness of an ancient document is to ask: even if we have confidence that what we have now is what was originally written down, did that original document give a true account of the things that happened, and the teachings spoken?

A key factor here is the shortness of the time between the claimed events and the document being produced and made public. If there is only a short gap, then living eyewitnesses (and their associates and immediate descendants) could verify or refute the claims made in the document.

The apostle Paul's letters (which mention, for example, the resurrection of Christ) were written within 20-30 years after Jesus' death (AD 30-33).

GOD 60 Hard Questions for Sceptics

Biblical Reliability

6, 7 Another method used to sort out the real from the mythical is to examine the actual contents of the document. These questions give examples of material that would not normally appear in mythical or propaganda writings.

Jesus Christ

Jesus Christ 13

Was Jesus just a good moral teacher and a faith healer – or is there more to Him than this?

3 Questions

1 What do you think was the most important theme in Jesus' teaching?

2 Was Jesus' death a tragic mistake?

3 Why do you think Jesus' resurrection is so emphasised by Christians?

13 Jesus Christ

'Jesus was just a good man – a prophet, maybe a healer, but not God.'

1 It is not generally noticed, but Jesus spoke a lot about . . . Himself. Who He was and what He had come to do were equal to if not more important than His moral teaching.

GOD 60 Hard Questions for Sceptics

In John's gospel this comes across particularly clearly. There, Jesus' miracles are referred to as 'signs' – pointers to His claim to be God incarnate. Jesus' challenge was not for people to improve their lives, but to come to Him.

2 To the consternation of the disciples, Jesus was constantly speaking about His death. Christians view Jesus' death as the ultimate purpose of His ministry, the planned goal of His mission.

3 The Christian faith relies on the truth of Jesus' resurrection. If He did not rise from the dead then all that Jesus said about Himself would be invalid. This would also cast doubt on His other teachings. Christians believe that the evidence for the resurrection is sound, and that there is no better explanation of the events recorded in the gospels.

Postscript
– The Final Question

It's important to how we live our lives that we think about what we believe and what we don't believe, and it's hoped that the questions will have helped you to assess how well different worldviews fit with reality.

But we are complex beings, and choosing what we believe is more than just an intellectual exercise. It's important to start with our minds, but ultimately our will and our emotions will play an equal if not a greater part in our decisions. We are not wholly rational creatures.

There's a story about a man who was convinced he was dead. His friends tried all manner of arguments to show that he was alive. Finally, one asked him the question, 'Do you think dead men bleed?'

'No,' replied the man.

At this the friend took the man's hand and used a pin to draw some blood. The man looked at the blood emerging from his finger. 'Goodness! So dead men do bleed, after all!'

For humans, there is a personal dimension to knowledge. In French there are two verbs for the English verb 'to know'. One is used about knowing facts, and the other is used to say that we know a person. Christians believe that God is a person, and we must 'know' Him this way. Rules and reasons have their part, but the core of the faith is about a relationship.

So, the final question is –

What is stopping you from knowing God today?

GOD 60 Hard Questions for Sceptics

Acknowledgements

Christians have been explaining and defending their faith for 2,000 years, and over that time many books of what is termed 'apologetics' have been written.

I have used some material from well-known historic sources – for example, Blaise Pascal, the seventeenth-century French scientist and mathematician, and, in the twentieth century, C. S. Lewis, the author and Oxford scholar. However, I have also referred to modern champions who tackle the questions asked most frequently today.

A useful and concise introduction is *The Ultimate Survival Guide*. For those wishing to read further I would recommend *But Is It Real?* by Amy Orr-Ewing and *The Reason for God* by Philip Keller.

A good online source is – *www.bethinking.org*.

Christian Vision for Men, *The Ultimate Survival Guide* (Malcolm Down, 2015)
Amy Orr-Ewing, *But Is It Real?* (InterVarsity Press, 2008)
Timothy Keller, *The Reason for God* (Hodder and Stoughton, 2009)

Notes

1. Terry Eagleton, 'Lunging, Failing, Mispunching': a review of Richard Dawkins' *The God Delusion* in *London Review of Books*, vol. 28, no. 20 – 19 Oct., 2006.
2. Quoted in Francis Collins, *The Language of God: A Scientist Presents Evidence for Belief* (Free Press, 2006), p. 75
3. *But Is It Real?* p. 50
4. R. T. France, 'The Gospels as Historical Sources for Jesus, The Founder of Christianity', *Truth* 1 (1985), p. 86.